Sho

Bristol & Bath

Nigel Vile

COUNTRYSIDE BOOKS
NEWBURY BERKSHIRE

First published 2024
© 2024 Nigel Vile

COUNTRYSIDE BOOKS
3 Catherine Road
Newbury, Berkshire, RG14 7NA

To view our complete range of books please visit us at
www.countrysidebooks.co.uk

ISBN 978 1 84674 432 7

All materials used in the manufacture of this book carry FSC certification.

Produced by The Letterworks Ltd., Reading
Designed and Typeset by KT Designs, St Helens
Printed by Holywell Press, Oxford

Introduction

I commented to an acquaintance that I was writing a book of short walks, adding as an aside that it is what we need as we get older. My younger friend replied that short walks are not just for those of more mature years. Not everybody has the time when working to spend hours and hours in the great outdoors. Equally, parents with young children might well struggle with walks of 5–10 miles. And, as I discovered at a conference in Cheltenham, there are many people out there who want short and gentle walks so that they can practise what is called 'mindful walking'.

This book will hopefully meet all of these needs, with each walk being between 2 and 4 miles in length. The aim also is to avoid main roads and to minimise the number of stiles. The majority of walks are relatively flat and easy, although I have included a few lofty hilltops, such is the nature of the terrain in this neck of the woods. Be assured, however, that there is nothing of Herculean proportions within these pages.

The Bristol and Bath region offers so much variety as is typified by the 20 walks in this book. There is the Severn Estuary and the Bristol Channel, explored on walks at Oldbury-on-Severn, Portishead and Clevedon. There are upland walks on the Mendip Hills at Crook Peak and Ebbor Gorge, as well as reservoirs and lakes at Chew and Litton. Both Bristol and Bath have green oases within their boundaries, explored on the urban trails in the book,

Short Walks near Bristol & Bath

all the better for the backdrop of hills in Bath and the dramatic Avon Gorge in Bristol.

North of these great cities lie the Cotswold Hills with their mellow stone villages that leave overseas visitors almost speechless. This landscape is explored on the walks at Marshfield and Hawkesbury Upton, drystone wall country where sheep farming provides an echo of the former West of England woollen trade. And there are the rivers, such as the Bristol Frome, explored on the walks at Iron Acton and Oldbury Court, not forgetting the River Avon that connects Bath and Bristol, followed on the walks at Freshford and Kelston.

Each walk comes with a short introduction, details on where to park, a description of the terrain, the relevant OS Explorer map, numbered directions and, of course, recommended places to eat and drink. I have enjoyed putting together this collection of walks, some old, some new, maybe some borrowed but hopefully nothing blue – to quote the old adage.

I wrote my first walking guidebook back in 1989, some 35 years ago. This will be my 35th walking guidebook in print – perfect symmetry. I can but wish you many hours of happy walking in this beautiful part of the world.

Nigel Vile

Publisher's Note

We hope that you obtain considerable enjoyment from this book; great care has been taken in its preparation. Although at the time of publication all routes followed public rights of way or permitted paths, diversion orders can be made and permissions withdrawn.

We cannot, of course, be held responsible for such diversion orders or any inaccuracies in the text which result from these or any other changes to the routes, nor any damage which might result from walkers trespassing on private property. We are anxious, though, that all the details covering the walks are kept up to date, and would therefore welcome information from readers which would be relevant to future editions.

The simple sketch maps that accompany the walks in this book are based on notes made by the author whilst surveying the routes on the ground. They are designed to show you how to reach the start and to point out the main features of the overall circuit, and they contain a progression of numbers that relate to the paragraphs of the text.

However, for the benefit of a proper map, we do recommend that you purchase the relevant Ordnance Survey sheet covering your walk. Ordnance Survey maps are widely available, especially through booksellers and local newsagents.

1 Oldbury-on-Severn

3 miles (4.8 km)

Start: The Anchor Inn, Church Lane, Oldbury-on-Severn. **Postcode:** BS35 1QA.

Parking: There is roadside parking alongside the pub, and opposite is a large car park if you plan on eating at the pub.

OS Map: Explorer 167 Thornbury, Dursley & Yate. **Grid Ref:** ST609923.

Terrain: A generally flat walk that follows tracks and riverside paths, with one short section of quiet road walking where dogs would need to be on leads. 1 stile with no dog gate.

Refreshments: The Anchor Inn serves excellent food in the traditional bar area, dining room, lounge and large attractive garden. The Oldbury-on-Severn Community Shop also has a café that is popular with walkers and cyclists.

WALK HIGHLIGHTS

A gentle stroll along flat paths that border the River Severn. The only climb, a very modest ascent, is onto a small knoll to reach St Arilda's Church in Oldbury. St Arilda was murdered, incidentally, for refusing to 'laye' with a

5

Short Walks near Bristol & Bath

local man called Municus back in the 5th century AD. From a churchyard seat, the views across the estuary are unrivalled. River estuaries are great places for birdwatching, and the Severn is no exception, with exact species depending upon tide times and the season of the year. The return to Oldbury follows a stretch of Oldbury Pill, an inlet used by the local sailing club for boat moorings, although when the tide is out the yachts are perched at perilous angles!

THE WALK

1 Facing the Anchor Inn, follow the road to the right as it climbs gently uphill to reach the local primary school beyond which is the entrance to St Arilda's Church. Enter the churchyard, walk around the church enjoying fine views of the Severn Estuary, before dropping downhill to a gate to rejoin the road. Follow the road ahead for 350m to a cul de sac lane on the right just past a house and bridleway.

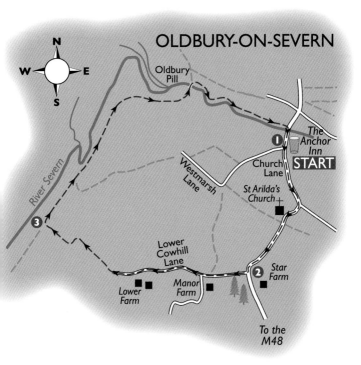

OLDBURY-ON-SEVERN

Oldbury Pill

River Severn

Westmarsh Lane

The Anchor Inn
START

Church Lane

St Arilda's Church

Lower Cowhill Lane

Lower Farm

Manor Farm

Star Farm

To the M48

2 Follow this lane for 650m until it ends by Lower Farm. Continue along a track for 600m to reach a gate before following the right edge of a field to a stile and the banks of the River Severn.

3 Follow the river to the right to reach a sluice complex on Oldbury Pill in 1.4km. Cross the sluice on a permissive path, turn right and drop down to the banks of Oldbury Pill. Follow this tidal stretch of waterway for 350m until it joins a road coming from the local sailing club. Follow this road ahead to the main road in Oldbury-on-Severn by the Anchor Inn.

2 Hawkesbury Upton & the Kilcott Valley

4 miles (6.4 km)

Start: Hawkesbury Upton Village Hall, High Street, Hawkesbury Upton. **Postcode:** GL9 1AU.
Parking: The Village Hall car park.
OS Map: Explorer 167 Thornbury, Dursley & Yate. **Grid Ref:** ST778870.
Terrain: Village lanes, footpaths and tracks. One moderate climb from the Kilcott Valley up to the Somerset Monument. No stiles so a good walk for dogs, but remember leads on the sections of quiet road walking.
Refreshments: The excellent Beaufort Arms, near the village hall, is a traditional pub with no frills or fuss.

WALK HIGHLIGHTS

Hawkesbury Upton stands on what is known colloquially as the 'Cotswold Edge' where the undulating plateau descends to the Severn Vale. That is a recipe for views! This walk from the village drops down through woodland and combes to the secretive Kilcott Valley before following a section of the Cotswold Way back up to the vast Somerset Monument, built by workers from the Badminton Estate to commemorate Lord Robert Edward Somerset who fought valiantly in the Peninsular War. Back in Hawkesbury Upton, the Beaufort Arms has won countless local CAMRA awards and is not to be missed.

THE WALK

1 Leave the car park, turn left, walking past the Beaufort Arms, to a junction at the end of Hawkesbury Upton's High Street just past the Fox Inn. Turn left along the road signposted to Starveall, keeping left at an early junction into Back Street. Follow this road as its winds its way out of the village to reach a road junction in 325m. Follow the footpath opposite that bears right down to a handgate and field. Continue across the field ahead, dropping downhill through three fields into a valley.

2 In a fourth field, continue to a small footbridge over a stream before following a track to the right down to a gate and wooded combe. Follow the grassy path through the bottom of this combe, ignoring occasional tracks that climb the adjoining hillsides, to reach a gate and the lane in the Kilcott Valley in 0.8km. Turn left and follow the lane for 550m to reach Mickley Cottage on the right. At this point, turn left and follow the Cotswold Way uphill, keeping left at a fork in 275m.

Short Walks near Bristol & Bath

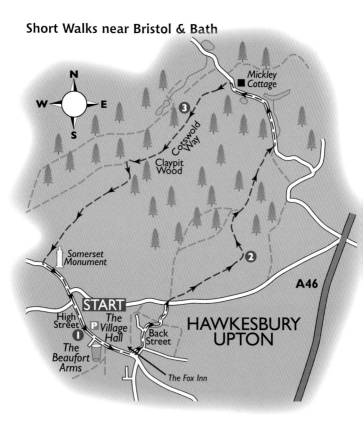

③ In 130m, pass through a gateway at the top of a climb into a hilltop field. Walk along the left edge of this field before entering Claypit Wood at the end of the field. Follow the path through this woodland for 250m before passing through a gateway on the left to follow a path up the left edge of a field. At the top of this field, turn right and follow the path for 0.8km to the Somerset Monument. Just before the monument, pass through a gateway on the left to follow a permissive path across the right edge of a field to join Hawkesbury Upton's High Street. Turn left to walk back to the car park.

3 Iron Acton, Frampton Cotterell & the Frome

4 miles (6.4 km)

Start: St James the Less Church, High Street, Iron Acton. **Postcode:** BS37 9UQ.

Parking: On Iron Acton's High Street in the vicinity of St James the Less Church.

OS Map: Explorer 167 Thornbury, Dursley & Yate. **Grid Ref:** ST681835.

Terrain: A flat and easy walk that follows little-used lanes and footpaths, including a section of the Frome Valley Walkway. Dogs would need to be on leads on the quiet lanes in case of the occasional vehicle.

Refreshments: Iron Acton has two good village pubs, the Lamb and the White Hart.

WALK HIGHLIGHTS

Explore two attractive villages in South Gloucestershire, just a few miles north of Bristol. Linking them is a section of the Frome Valley Walkway, a pleasant riverside path that follows the (Bristol) Frome from its source in Dodington

Short Walks near Bristol & Bath

Park through to Bristol's city centre. Other points of interest along the way include secluded green lanes, old iron workings and an associated tramline, a manor house and deciduous woodland in the shape of Chill Wood. This walk takes you through a delightful rural oasis in an area that has been subsumed by so much modern development.

THE WALK

1 With your back to the church, turn left and walk the whole length of the High Street to a junction in front of the White Hart Inn. Turn left and, in 230m, where the main road bears right keep ahead along a side turning passing in front of the gabled Home Close. In 180m, having crossed a railway line, turn right to begin following the Frome Valley Walkway, just past the entrance to Algars Manor. Walk the length of a narrow field to a gate, before following a riverside path alongside the garden of a property to a gate and an old mineral railway. Turn left, cross the Frome and turn right to follow a winding enclosed path down to a field. Continue following the Frome Valley Walkway alongside the river, often hidden in bushes to the right, for 1.2km to a footbridge on the right, ignoring an earlier concrete bridge on the right that accesses the B4058.

2 Cross the Frome, and follow a path to the left through the woodland bordering the river for 325m until the path enters an open field. Walking in the same direction, pass through a gateway in the bushes in 175m and enter open grassland known as the Centenary Fields. Cross this field to a gate by some allotments to join a back lane in Frampton End. Continue ahead before turning left just before a rank of cottages and Frampton Church. Follow a drive down to a bridge over the Frome before entering a small paddock. Walk down the right edge of this paddock to a gate before following an enclosed path between horse paddocks to a handgate opposite at the entrance to woodland. Climb some steps beyond this gate to reach the bed of a former mineral line, turn left and follow the track bed for 120m to a gap in the hedge on the right. Walk ahead across a field, with woodland on the right. Where the woodland ends, continue across the field to a gate opposite, cross the following field to the next gate and then cross one final field to a gate and stile to the left of some properties and join a lane (Frampton End Road).

3 Turn left and follow this quiet winding lane for 1.2km through to the edge of Iron Acton just before Algars Manor. Before crossing the Frome, turn right to follow another section of the Frome Valley Walkway. Follow the Frome

Walk 3 – **Iron Acton, Frampton Cotterell & the Frome**

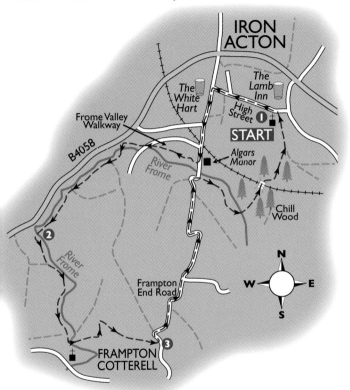

upstream to a weir and sluices, cross the river and enter Chill Wood. Follow the path through the woodland to a gate at the exit from the trees and an open field. Follow the left edge of this field for 75m, turn left and climb up some steps to cross the Thornbury Railway. Descend the far side of the embankment and follow a path across open grassland across to a gate and track at the back of some houses. Turn left and follow an enclosed path back to Iron Acton Church.

4 Portishead & the Bristol Channel

2¾ miles (4.4 km)

Start: Portishead Open Air Pool, Esplanade Rd, Portishead, North Somerset. **Postcode:** BS20 7HD.
Parking: On Esplanade Road by the Open Air Pool.
OS Map: Explorer 154 Bristol West & Portishead. **Grid Ref:** ST465775.
Terrain: Footpaths, woodland, some suburban pavements and traffic-free paths around a modern marina. This is not really a dog-friendly walk unless dogs are happy to be on leads for much of the walk.
Refreshments: There is a community café at Portishead Open Pool that is open from April to October. Or, for an authentic taste of the sea, visit Sea Rock on Portishead's Marina, an excellent fish and chips restaurant or take away to eat on the quay.

WALK HIGHLIGHTS

The walk starts from Portishead's open air swimming pool, so plan for a dip if the weather is good. After exploring the foreshore of the Mouth of the Severn, the walk heads through pleasant open spaces and suburban roads to the town's marina, formerly used for importing coal from Wales in order to supply the local power station. Yachts and lavish apartments, a pier and a lifeboat station are some of the points of interest. It is then back along the coast passing East Wood before a detour to Battery Point. This headland overlooking the Bristol Channel is the closest point on UK mainland passed by ocean going ships, in this case huge vessels making for the local docks at Portbury and Avonmouth.

THE WALK

❶ With the Open Air Pool on your right, walk along Esplanade Road for 400m, keeping the Mouth of the Severn on the right and the marine lake to your left. When you reach the sailing club on your left, head down steps and follow the path round to the right to cross a footbridge over the lake by the children's playground. Walk across the large open area of grassland ahead, the local cricket pitch, to a gap to the right of the cricket pavilion, detouring around the boundary if play is taking place. Beyond the pavilion, follow Rodmoor Road uphill to its junction with Beach Road West. Turn left to a crossroads by Vale Vets. Cross over into Beach Road East and continue to the next junction by a mini roundabout. Continue opposite along what is still Beach Road East down to the A369 Station Road.

❷ Cross over and follow the road to the right past the local primary school towards the Parish Wharf Leisure Centre. Just before the leisure centre, follow a path on the left down to Portishead Marina. Turn right to the end of the marina, turn left and follow the far end of the marina past some apartments for 75m. Turn left and follow the eastern side of the marina past a large lock that gives access to the Mouth of the Severn. Cross the lock on a bridge, turn right and follow the waterside path past La Marina Restaurant along to an old pier looking out onto the Severn. Turn left, passing the local lifeboat station.

❸ Climb a stepped path ahead up to the Royal Inn and follow the road ahead past the pub before turning right onto a very quiet lane signposted as the North Somerset Tidal Trail. Follow this lane as it runs alongside East Wood for 700m to a point where it bears left to begin climbing uphill; to

Short Walks near Bristol & Bath

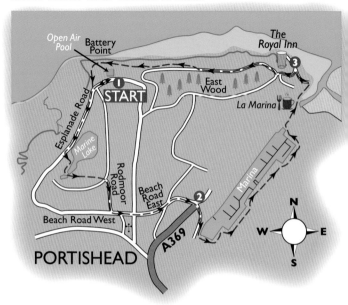

the right is the gated entrance to properties called Tallis House and the Saltings. At this point, veer right onto a path that passes through woodland to reach an open headland. Walk across this headland before following a stepped path to the left, just past the Open Air Pool, down to Esplanade Road – although the detour ahead to Battery Point will no doubt prove irresistible.

5 Clifton Downs & Avon Gorge

3½ miles (5.6 km)

Start: The Downs Café, Stoke Road, Durdham Downs, Bristol.
  Postcode: BS9 1FG.
Parking: There is 5-hours-free roadside parking by the Downs Café.
OS Map: Explorer 155 Bristol & Bath. **Grid Ref:** ST571750.
Terrain: An undulating walk, a combination of the open Downs, where
  dogs can run free, and wide tarmac footpaths that border roads,
  where leads would be necessary. No stiles and very popular dog-
  walking country for Bristolians.
Refreshments: The walk starts from the Downs Café, with its excellent
  outdoor seating area overlooking … the Downs! Halfway around the
  walk is the 360 Café at the Observatory with an excellent rooftop
  terrace.

WALK HIGHLIGHTS

The Downs is a huge expanse of protected parkland bordering Clifton Village, Clifton and the Redland areas of Bristol. This walk starts from the Downs Café by the landmark Water Tower, built in 1954 to improve water pressure in the city, before exploring an area known as 'The Dumps'. This is a site of deep trenches that may well have been lead workings dating from the 17th century. It is onwards to the Observatory, with its 360 degree Camera Obscura, by way of the gentile and tree-lined Promenade, before some spectacular views of the Avon Gorge and Brunel's Suspension Bridge as the walk heads to a viewpoint called Sea Walls. The heart of the Downs, this urban 'green lung', is explored as the walk returns to the welcome sight of the Downs Café.

Short Walks near Bristol & Bath

THE WALK

1 From the Downs Café, just along the road from the Water Tower, cross the road onto the Downs. Walk ahead towards an uneven area of ground, covered in bushes, known as 'The Dumps'. Follow the path through these bushes until, 700m on from the start of the walk, you reach an access road leading to the Downs Council Depot on the right. Follow a path to the left of the entrance to this depot, the busy A4176 nearby to the left, which drops down to join a major road junction in 400m where Clifton Down Road joins Bridge Valley Road.

2 Cross over and follow a tree-lined avenue to the right signposted to Clifton Village, amongst other places. Follow this avenue, known as 'The Promenade', for 450m to a junction, with grand mansions on the opposite side of the road. Take the left-hand path that borders the road and, in 150m, at the next junction, turn right on a path signposted to 'The Observatory'. Walk up to this noted landmark, passing to its left, to follow a path high above the Avon Gorge with a fine view of Brunel's Suspension Bridge. Continue on the path as it winds its way back to rejoin 'The Promenade' in 200m.

3 Retrace your steps back along the Promenade to the major road junction passed earlier and cross over into Fountains Hill. In 250m, at the top of a gentle climb on paths that border the road, turn left into Circular Road. Follow any of the paths that border this road for 1.3km to a fine viewpoint above the Avon Gorge known as 'Sea Walls'. Having enjoyed the views, cross the road and walk across the open Downs opposite making for the

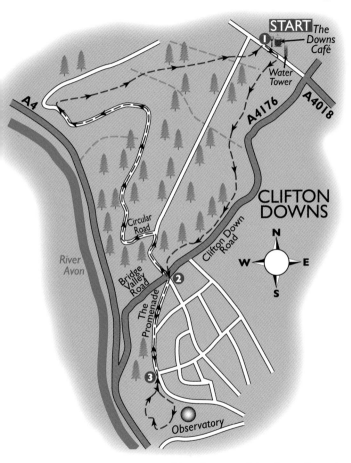

clearly visible Water Tower, some 1100m distant, and the chance for rest and refreshment at the Downs Café.

6 Oldbury Court, Frenchay & the Frome Valley

2½ miles (4 km)

Start: Oldbury Court Car Park, Oldbury Court, Fishponds, Bristol.
   Postcode: BS16 2JW.
Parking: Oldbury Court Car Park; fee payable.
OS Map: Explorer 155 Bristol & Bath. **Grid Ref:** ST635766.
Terrain: An uneven path alongside the River Frome; one short climb uphill onto Frenchay Common. One stile; dogs will need to be on their leads on the roads around Frenchay. The Oldbury Court Estate is prime dog-walking country.
Refreshments: The White Lion on Frenchay Common is a Greene King pub with a good menu and outdoor seating. There is also a refreshment kiosk by the car park at Oldbury Court, plus a seasonal ice cream seller.

WALK HIGHLIGHTS

Oldbury Court, a former landed estate, is now one of the City of Bristol's finest parks that includes what was once an arboretum. Below, in a wooded gorge, flows the River Frome on its course from Dodington Park to Bristol's city centre. Nearby Frenchay boasts many handsome Georgian houses located around one of the finest village commons in the area, the whole scene overlooked by Frenchay Church. When playing cricket on the Common, local hero W.G.Grace once smashed the church clock when hitting a six! This is a surprisingly rural excursion considering the close proximity to Bristol.

THE WALK

❶ Walk back to the car park entrance and follow the path to the right down past the children's play area and, in another 75m, drop down some steps on the right. At a junction at the bottom of the steps, turn left and continue downhill for 200m to reach the River Frome. Turn right and follow the river upstream, the path becoming uneven, to reach Frenchay Bridge in 850m. Cross the bridge, turn left and walk up Pearces Hill. Near the top of the hill, turn right and walk along to the White Lion.

❷ Beyond the pub, turn left along Westbourne Terrace, then head onto the common, passing the local primary school on your right to reach Frenchay Parish Church. Keep ahead along the road in front of the church to reach a junction with Beckspool Road. Cross to the pavement opposite and follow this road to the right for 300m to Cedar Hall, passing Frenchay's Unitarian Church along the way. Cross the road to a handgate opposite before following a path across the next field to another handgate. Beyond this gate, ignore the path directly ahead; instead follow the path to its right and walk across to a seat. Continue following this path to the right and on downhill passing the end of some woodland to a gate and a NT Frenchay Moor sign.

Short Walks near Bristol & Bath

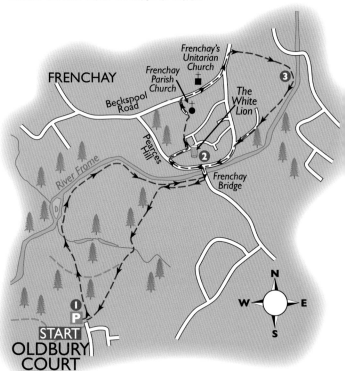

③ Follow a path to the right between paddocks to reach a stile before following Chapel Lane to its junction with Frenchay Hill. Turn left and walk along to Frenchay Bridge. Cross the bridge and turn right but, rather than following the riverside path signposted to Snuff Mills, follow the path to the left uphill signposted to Oldbury Court Road. In 550m cross a small stream and, in another 50m, keep left at a fork. Continue along the path through the Oldbury Court Estate back to the children's play area before turning left back to the car park.

7 Dyrham & Hinton Hill

2½ miles (4 km)

Start: Lower Street in Dyrham, accessed from the A46 on an unclassified road 800m south of the main entrance to the National Trust's Dyrham Park property. **Postcode:** SN14 8EU.

Parking: There is parking on the roadside in Lower Street, but do be considerate towards local residents.

OS Map: Explorer 155 Bristol & Bath. **Grid Ref:** ST739756.

Terrain: Quiet lanes and footpaths, with one climb up Cock Hill early in the walk. There are gates rather than stiles which makes this a dog-friendly walk, although leads will be necessary for the first part of the walk on those quiet lanes.

Refreshments: There are no refreshment facilities on the walk itself but, if you are a member of the National Trust, there is a 'back door' entrance into Dyrham Park where you will find a tearoom as well as an outdoor refreshment kiosk. Details in the directions but do carry your membership card.

Short Walks near Bristol & Bath

WALK HIGHLIGHTS

From a handsome Cotswold village with a grand National Trust property to a hillfort with a view. The hillfort on Hinton Hill, also known as Dyrham Camp, was the scene in AD 577 of a decisive battle between the Saxons and the Ancient Britons. The victorious Saxons gained control over Cirencester, Gloucester and Bath and drove the Ancient Britons back to Wales and Somerset. The view extends beyond the Severn Vale towards the Forest of Dean and the Welsh Hills. And even if you are not a National Trust member, there is still the chance to visit St Peter's Church that overlooks Dyrham House and its grounds. For NT members, there is a 'back door' into the grounds.

THE WALK

1 Walk down Lower Street to a T-junction before turning right on a road signposted to Hinton. Ignoring a right turn in 300m, continue along the road for 350m to a junction by Talbot Farm. Turn right and walk up Cock Lane for 600m to the next junction. Turn right and, in 30m, bear right onto a footpath.

2 Ahead is Hinton Hill, the site of an ancient hillfort. Bear left and climb to the top of this hill before dropping down to a gap in the bottom right corner of this hilltop enclosure, just to the right of one of the hillfort's ramparts. Walk down the right edge of the following field to a gate before walking across the open field ahead to join the Cotswold Way just below the boundary wall of Dyrham Park. If the open field is blocked by crops, simply turn right and follow the right edge of the field to join the Cotswold Way.

3 Turn right and follow the Cotswold Way along the left edges of four fields to a gate and track. Follow this track and, immediately before it joins a road in Dyrham, turn left onto an ancient paved path. Follow this path for 100m along to a path on the left leading to St Peter's Church. Walk along to the church and back before rejoining the road in Dyrham. Turn left, walk along past the rear entrance to Dyrham Park to a junction by a small green before turning right back into Dyrham's main street.

NOTE: On the path back from the church, a gate on the left gives access to Dyrham Park for card carrying members of the National Trust.

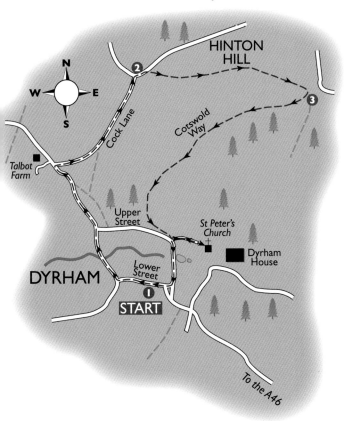

8 Marshfield & the Southwolds

3¾ miles (6 km)

Start: The Almshouses, High Street, Marshfield. **Postcode:** SN14 8LX.
Parking: There is roadside parking alongside the Almshouses.
OS Map: Explorer 155 Bristol & Bath. **Grid Ref:** ST774737.
Terrain: An undulating walk, mainly on very quiet country lanes that border sheep pasture enclosed by classic drystone walls. The walk is fine for dogs but they will need to be kept on leads due to the very occasional vehicle.
Refreshments: The Catherine Wheel in Marshfield is passed just before the end of the walk and has a good reputation. There is also the Lord Nelson which is located in Marshfield's Market Place or a teashop called Sweetapples on the High Street.

WALK HIGHLIGHTS

Marshfield once lay on the main London to Bristol coach road, later the main A420. There came a bypass and the M4 so now its many handsome cottages and grand houses line a much quieter High Street that is so long that a Mummer's play is held along its length each Boxing Day with no fewer than half a dozen scenes at various locations. To the north lies an undulating Cotswold landscape of archetypal sheep pasture and drystone walls, as well as the unusual Castle Farm. Writing in *Countryfile* magazine, Fergus Collins describes this area as his favourite part of the Cotswolds on account of its lack of commercialism; 'an area that few people visit giving it a more authentic feel'.

THE WALK

❶ With your back to the almshouses, follow the High Street to the right for 150m before turning right onto a back lane to walk up to the A420. Cross with care and follow Bond's Lane opposite for 500m down to a junction by Westend Farm. Follow the cul de sac lane opposite for 375m until it ends at Westend Town Farm.

❷ Continue along the track ahead, ignoring one tempting right turn, to cross Broadmead Brook in 350m. Continue along the track, shown as Brookhouse

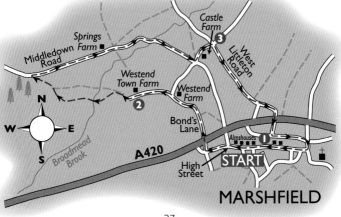

Short Walks near Bristol & Bath

Lane on the OS map, to join Middledown Road in 600m. Follow this road to the right for 700m to reach Springs Farm before continuing for another 800m to a crossroads just before Castle Farm. Turn left to a crossroads in 200m before turning right onto West Littleton Road.

3 Follow this road for 800m to the A420, ignoring a right turn 200m earlier. Cross over and follow West Littleton Road opposite for 150m to its junction with Back Lane in Marshfield. Turn left and follow Back Lane for 300m to a junction before turning right down to Marshfield's Market Place by Davis Meade Estate Agent and the Lord Nelson pub. Turn right and walk the whole length of the High Street, some 750m, back to the almshouses, passing Sweetapples Teashop and the Catherine Wheel pub along the way.

9 Corsham

4 miles (6.4 km)

Start: Lacock Road Car Park, Lacock Road, Corsham.
  Postcode: SN13 9QG.
Parking: Lacock Road Car Park.
OS Map: Explorer 156 Chippenham & Bradford-on-Avon.
  Grid Ref: ST881702.
Terrain: A flat and easy walk around Corsham and its environs. There are stiles and cattle between Westrop and Easton, avoidable if you have a dog by following the quiet lane shown on the map. Dogs will, of course, have to be on leads, as they will in Corsham Park which is prime sheep-grazing country.
Refreshments: There are several pubs and cafés on Corsham's High Street. A particular favourite is the Flemish Weaver, whose name harks back to Corsham's heyday as a textile centre.

Short Walks near Bristol & Bath

WALK HIGHLIGHTS

Corsham Court, a grand stately home, is one of the finest country houses in Wiltshire. Alongside lies the manicured parkland of Corsham Park, designed and laid out in 1759 by Lancelot Brown. The centrepiece of the park is Corsham Lake, where ornithologists will find many species including grebes and teal, shoveler and gadwall, not forgetting the ubiquitous Canada geese. The walk also visits the neighbouring hamlets of Westrop and Easton, as well as providing the opportunity to explore Corsham itself, a handsome place with independent shops, pubs and cafés and an excellent visitor centre.

THE WALK

1 Cross the Lacock Road to a gate, follow an enclosed path to another gate and enter Corsham Park. Walk ahead for 10m, turn right and follow a path to a gate at the far end of Corsham Park. Beyond this gate, walk ahead and follow an enclosed signposted path to a gate and field. Cross this field to a gate and lane. Turn left and follow the lane for 275m through Eastrop. Immediately before property number 14, turn right along a drive and walk up to a stile. Keep ahead to the next stile before walking across to the far left corner of a much larger field. Cross a stone slab stile, turn right and follow the right edge of a field along to a stile and an enclosed path down to the lane in Easton.

2 Turn left and walk through Easton. At the far end of the village, having passed Easton Farm, continue along the lane for 100m to a signposted path on the left. Cross a stile and walk across a field to a gateway opposite before walking across a second field to a stile in its far right corner. Join a lane, turn left and continue for 675m down to the main A4. Just before this main road, pass through a gate on the left and walk across Corsham Park to a gate in the middle of the end field boundary. In the following field, walk up to a gate in the far left-hand corner. Pass through a belt of trees and, in the following field, keep ahead to the next gate in 40m.

3 Walk down the right edge of the field ahead to a gate in its bottom right corner in 575m. Follow the right edge of the following field to the next gate, before following the right edge of one final field around to Corsham Church. Walk through the churchyard and down Church Street to Corsham's High Street. Turn left and, in 150m, just before Post Office

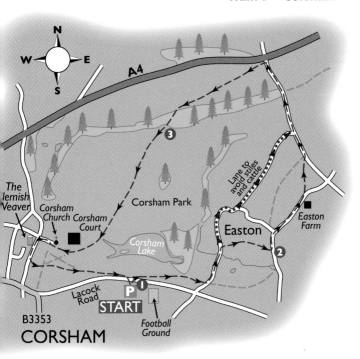

Lane and a Chinese restaurant on the right, turn left along a back alley that leads to a tree-lined avenue called South Avenue. Cross this avenue to a gate and Corsham Park. Walk ahead across the Park for 650m to reach some oak trees by Corsham Lake. Just past these trees, turn right and walk up to a gate in the top boundary of Corsham Park. Beyond this gate, retrace your steps back to Lacock Road and the car park.

10 Bathampton, Batheaston & the Meadows

3 miles (4.8 km)

Start: Batheaston Car Park, London Road East, Batheaston.
  Postcode: BA1 7NB.
Parking: The public car park in Batheaston opposite the local shops.
OS Map: Explorer 155 Bristol & Bath. **Grid Ref:** ST780674.
Terrain: A generally flat walk that follows field paths and canal
  towpath, with 500m of pavement walking at the beginning and a
  quiet lane as the walk enters Bathampton where dogs would need
  to be on leads. No stiles. The riverside meadows can be muddy
  following heavy rainfall.
Refreshments: The George Inn is a popular Chef & Brewer pub
  located on the banks of the Kennet & Avon Canal with plenty of
  outside seating. Alternatively, try Gather Café & Bar in Batheaston,
  where breakfast and lunch are served as well as some very enticing
  cakes.

WALK HIGHLIGHTS

Batheaston, on the western outskirts of Bath, is a much better place following the construction of a bypass in 1995. Prior to this date, its main street had been the traffic clogged A4. From the village, the walk crosses nearby meadowland to reach neighbouring Bathampton where the excellent George Inn sits alongside the Kennet & Avon Canal. Towpath walking follows before a footpath that crosses Bathampton Meadows brings the walk back to Batheaston. It is incredible to think that the council recently wanted to build a park-and-ride on these meadows, a beautiful landscape surrounded by hills on all sides – Brown's Folly Reserve, Solsbury Hill, Lansdown Hill and Bathampton Down.

THE WALK

❶ Leave the car park and turn right along London Road East. In 500m, just before a roundabout at the eastern end of the Batheaston Bypass, turn right down towards the entrance to a series of apartments called Avondale before turning left onto a footpath that passes under the bypass. Emerge onto a main road, turn right and walk under a railway bridge before following a footpath on the right signposted to Bathampton.

❷ Cross the Avon, the main London railway on your right, before dropping down to a handgate and meadow. Walk diagonally across the middle of this field towards some housing to reach a gate. Keep ahead to another gate, cross a railway line and follow the lane ahead into Bathampton. In 300m, turn left to join the Kennet & Avon Canal and follow the towpath to the right. In 1.2km, just before bridge 184, veer right on a path that climbs up from the towpath to a quiet lane. Turn right, cross a railway line before following a footpath signposted to the left along to a gate and field.

❸ Turn right and walk down the right edge of a field to a footbridge. Beyond this bridge, turn right and follow a path that passes under the Batheaston Bypass. Beyond the bypass, follow a path that follows the line of electricity wires across a field to a gate and driveway. Follow this driveway to the left along to the Bathampton to Batheaston road. Turn right for a few paces, cross the road and opposite is a recently created path that will return you to Batheaston and the car park by way of the River Avon.

Short Walks near Bristol & Bath

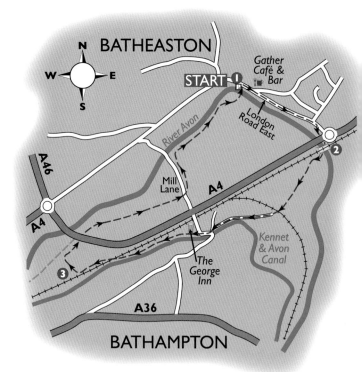

11 Bath

3 miles (4.8 km)

Start: Bath Abbey's West Door, Bath. **Postcode:** BA1 1LT.

Parking: There are many car parks in Bath's city centre but all are expensive so the best advice is to use one of three park-and-ride facilities into the city. These are at Lansdown, Odd Down and Newbridge. Alternatively, Bath is served by excellent bus and train services.

OS Map: Explorer 155 Bristol & Bath. **Grid Ref:** ST751647.

Terrain: A generally flat walk that follows pavements, canal towpath and grassy paths. One climb up onto Bathwick Hill and the view. Unsuitable for dogs.

Refreshments: A whole book could be written on where to eat and drink in Bath but, for a real flavour of the city, visit Sally Lunn's on North Parade Passage, home of the 'Bath Bun', a regional speciality now known the world over. The actual building dates from 1482 and claims to be the oldest house in Bath.

Short Walks near Bristol & Bath

WALK HIGHLIGHTS
A walk that takes in a selection of Bath's finest architecture – the Abbey, Pulteney Bridge, Great Pulteney Street, the Holburne Museum and Sydney Gardens. There is also a finely crafted section of the K&A Canal, with ornate bridges and sculptured stonework designed to appease local landowners in the 18th century opposed to the M4 of its day. The walk climbs uphill onto the open green spaces of Bathwick Hill bringing one of the finest views across the city. References in the directions to 'Bog Island' relate to a former underground set of toilets, that subsequently became the notorious 1980s 'Island Club'.

THE WALK
❶ Facing Bath Abbey, bear right across Abbey Churchyard to reach York Street. Turn left along York Street before crossing 'Bog Island' to reach Pierrepont Street and the balustrades above Parade Gardens. Turn left, the Avon below on the right, towards Pulteney Bridge. Cross Pulteney Bridge and walk the length of Great Pulteney Street to reach the A36. Cross over and follow the road that runs to the right of the Holburne Museum. Once past the museum, turn left into Sydney Gardens and walk across to a pillared folly. Continue across a railway bridge and, just before the next bridge, look out for a white iron gateway that gives access to the Kennet & Avon Canal. Turn right and, after passing through a tunnel, go up some steps on the right and cross the canal to continue along its opposite bank. On reaching a boat basin, climb a cobbled path on the left to reach Bathwick Hill.

❷ Cross the road to find a stepped path opposite by a supermarket to rejoin the canal's towpath. Continue to a lock, cross a bridge and walk up to a road called Sydney Buildings. Cross over and follow a stepped path up onto Bathwick Meadow. Follow the tarmac path ahead for 550m up the side of the meadow, ignoring gates on the right that access the meadow itself, to reach a seat at the top of a climb. Walk past this seat for a few paces before following a path on the right downhill for 150m to a stile on the right. Beyond this stile, follow a grassy path through three gates by Richens Orchard. After the third gate, continue across the hillside for 75m into a dip, bear left and drop downhill to a gate and Sydney Buildings.

❸ Turn right and, in 225m, turn left down a lane to re-cross the Kennet &

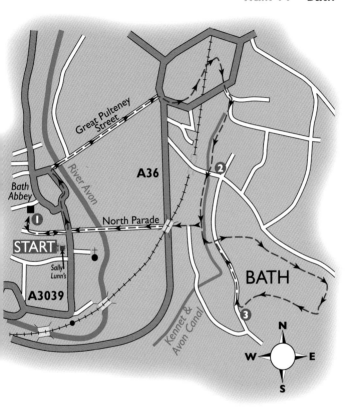

Avon Canal. Follow the towpath to the right for 100m, descend some steps on the left, pass under a railway bridge to reach the A36. Follow North Parade opposite and, having crossed the River Avon, re-cross 'Bog Island' to follow York Street back to the abbey. Alternatively, a brief detour will bring you to North Parade Passage and the iconic Sally Lunn's.

12 Freshford & the Avon Valley

4 miles (6.4 km)

Start: The Inn at Freshford, The Hill, Freshford. **Postcode:** BA2 7WG.
Parking: There is roadside parking alongside the pub or just along the
   road past the medieval Freshford Bridge. Alternatively, take the train
   to Freshford Station and start the walk from there.
OS Map: Explorer 155 Bristol & Bath and 156 Chippenham &
   Bradford-on-Avon. **Grid Ref:** ST791600.
Terrain: A generally flat walk that follows field paths and canal
   towpath, with two short sections of quiet road walking where dogs
   would need to be on leads. Three stiles without dog gates.
Refreshments: There are plenty of options on this walk. The Inn
   at Freshford, the Cross Guns at Avoncliff, No 10 Tea Garden at
   Avoncliff, and the Hop Pole at Limpley Stoke are all passed along
   the route.

WALK HIGHLIGHTS

Freshford's wealth was founded upon the West of England cloth trade.
Today, the grand houses of the former mill owners and the cottages of
the weavers are in high demand in this picturesque village just south of

Bath. The River Avon is followed through to Avoncliff, where John Rennie's vast aqueduct carrying the K&A across the river dominates the village. A pleasant section of the canal is followed through the wooded Avon Valley, with one local guidebook describing the setting as 'sylvan and resplendent'. The return is by way of Limpley Stoke, another handsome village, and if the area looks familiar, it was the location for much of the 1953 English film *The Titfield Thunderbolt* starring Sid James and Stanley Holloway. A timeless classic.

THE WALK

❶ With your back to the Inn at Freshford, follow the road to the right across Freshford Bridge and the River Frome. Immediately past the bridge, pass through a handgate on the left and walk diagonally across the middle of a large field to a gate in its far right corner. Continue along a path that runs between the River Avon and Avoncliff Wood to the next gate, before crossing a riverside meadow to another gate. Follow an enclosed path to the next handgate before continuing along an access drive into Avoncliff, passing Ancliff Square along the way.

❷ Upon reaching Number 10 Tea Garden, climb some steps up to the Kennet & Avon Canal, turn left and cross Avoncliff Aqueduct. Turn left and

Short Walks near Bristol & Bath

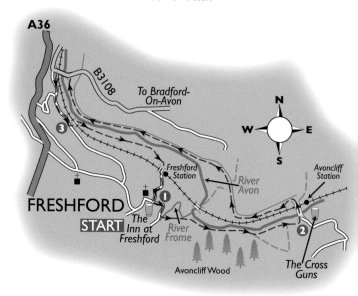

follow the towpath for 2.4km and, where the towpath bears right towards Winsley Hill, cross a semi-hidden stile in the hedgerow on the left. Turn right to a gate and stile before crossing a field to a stile and the busy B3108. Turn left, cross the River Avon on Stokeford Bridge, pass under a railway bridge and turn left into Lower Stoke. Follow this road through Limpley Stoke for 500m, passing the Hop Pole Inn, to reach the foot of Crowe Hill.

❸ Turn left, follow a track down to a railway bridge and gate and a field by the River Avon. Turn right and follow a footpath across the top right edges of two fields. Keep ahead in a third field, passing to the right of Freshford Sewage Treatment Plant, to join the plant's access track. Follow this track ahead and to the right up to Freshford Station. Cross the bridge over the railway and follow Station Road along to its junction with Church Hill. Turn left to return to the Inn at Freshford.

13 Monkton Combe & Midford

2¾ miles (4.4 km)

Start: Monkton Combe Church, Church Lane, Monkton Combe.
  Postcode: BA2 7EX.
Parking: There is a small car park opposite the church. There is also
  limited roadside parking on Church Lane.
OS Map: Explorer 155 Bristol & Bath. **Grid Ref:** ST772619.
Terrain: A quiet lane, a railway path and a disused canal on what is a
  flat and easy walk other than a steep stepped path up onto the
  former railway. No stiles, but dogs will need to be on leads on
  the section of road walking and on the railway path which is shared
  with cyclists.
Refreshments: The Wheelwrights Arms in Monkton Combe, or sister
  pub, the Hope & Anchor in Midford is passed half-way round
  the route.

WALK HIGHLIGHTS

Two villages south of Bath, once connected by the Somerset Coal Canal
and subsequently the Somerset & Dorset Railway. The decaying remains
of the canal are followed on this walk, as is a section of the Somerset &

Short Walks near Bristol & Bath

Dorset Railway that is now a shared-use path. There is also the secretive Tucking Mill Reservoir, as well as William Smith's cottage. Smith, the father of British geology, lived this way when working as the canal's engineer. He was immortalised in Simon Winchester's book, *The Map that Changed the World*, the map being the first geological map of Britain, although Winchester points out discrepancies in what actual property Smith lived in.

THE WALK

1 Walk through the churchyard, passing the grave of Harry Patch, the last surviving World War I veteran, to a gate and lane (Tucking Mill Lane). Follow this lane to the left for 850m into Tucking Mill. Immediately past Tucking Mill Cottage on your right, turn right and follow a footpath up past Tucking Mill Reservoir before climbing some steps on the left up to the former Somerset & Dorset Railway, now a shared-use path.

2 Follow the former railway to the left for 1km to the car park by the Hope & Anchor pub in Midford. Drop down to the B3110, turn left, pass the pub and, in a few paces, having crossed the portal of a former canal bridge, turn left onto a public footpath.

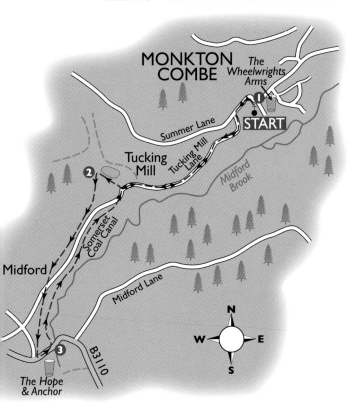

❸ Beyond a fenced-in section of path, continue along what was the towpath of the Somerset Coal Canal, the ditch on the left being the former canal. Follow the former towpath for 1km to reach the lane in front of Tucking Mill Cottage. Follow this lane to the right, retracing the initial section of the walk, for 1km back to Monkton Combe Church and the car park.

14 Kelston & the River Avon

3 miles (4.8 km)

Start: Church Lane, Kelston, a cul de sac turning off the main A431 Bath to Bristol road by Tower House. **Postcode:** BA1 9AG.

Parking: There is ample roadside parking in Church Lane. The walk could start from the Bath Soft Cheese Company's car park but this can be full due to the popularity of the café and shop.

OS Map: Explorer 155 Bristol & Bath. **Grid Ref:** ST698669.

Terrain: A flat and easy walk with gates rather than stiles. Dogs should be kept on their leads on the short section of road-walking in Kelston and around the Cheese Shop and Café. There can be cattle in one or two fields.

Refreshments: The Bath Soft Cheese Company's café serves breakfasts, lunches and afternoon teas. An almost obligatory lunch is 'The Ploughman's' with two award winning cheeses, salad, homemade piccalilli, apple and crusty bread. Booking is strongly advised at busy times.

WALK HIGHLIGHTS

The Bath Soft Cheese Company has earned a nationwide reputation for its fine products. Having passed its excellent shop and café, this walk heads across to Kelston Mills. The mills here were brass mills where it is alleged the noise of the hammers inspired some of the louder passages in Handel's 'Hallelujah Chorus'. A pleasant stroll along the banks of the River Avon follows, along to Salford Marina with its collection of pleasure boats, before field paths head back to Kelston and a well-deserved cheese ploughman's lunch, before a short stroll back to Church Lane.

THE WALK

❶ Walk back up to the A431 and turn left. In 200m, immediately before Kelston Forge and a disused telephone box, turn left down a side lane. Follow this lane, which becomes a footpath, for 175m to a gate and junction of paths by the Bath Soft Cheese complex. Follow the path to the right signposted to Kelston Mills and, beyond a gate, cross a drive to another gate and continue into a field. Walk across to the far bottom right-hand corner of this field, pass through a gateway and follow a track for 175m to join a lane. Follow this lane ahead into Kelston Mills.

❷ At a junction in the centre of the village, keep left before walking in front of a rank of three-storey properties to reach a gate. Turn right and walk

Short Walks near Bristol & Bath

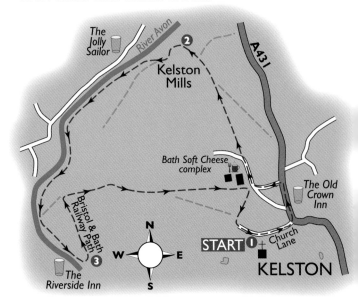

down the right edge of a field to reach the River Avon. Pass through a gate on the left and follow the river upstream for 1km to reach a former railway bridge. Pass under this bridge and continue following the Avon upstream for 500m to reach a lock opposite the Riverside Inn. Turn left and follow an enclosed path up to the Bristol & Bath Railway Path.

❸ Turn left and follow the Railway Path for 325m before veering right onto a footpath that drops down the railway embankment to a gate and track. Follow this track to the left for just over 800m to reach some farm buildings, before continuing along an enclosed footpath to the right of these buildings to reach a junction of paths, the Bath Soft Cheese complex to the left. Follow the enclosed path to the right signposted to 'The Church'. Pass through a gateway in 200m, cross a paddock to another gateway and continue along the back lane ahead that soon bears left up into Church Lane.

15 Litton's Secret Reservoirs

2¼ miles (3.6 km)

Start: The Litton, Litton, Near Wells. **Postcode:** BA3 4PW.
Parking: Park at the far end of the Litton's car park, by a horse
  chestnut tree. If you do not intend to eat and drink at the Litton,
  park on Litton Lane, a turning on the right just past this destination
  pub if coming from the A39.
OS Map: Explorer 141 Cheddar Gorge & Mendip Hills West.
  Grid Ref: ST594545.
Terrain: A flat and easy walk with just one gentle climb from the
  Lower Reservoir to the Upper Reservoir at Litton's Reservoirs. One
  slightly awkward stile just beyond the Upper Reservoir would make
  this walk difficult for larger dogs.
Refreshments: The Litton is an award-winning country pub and
  boutique hotel, where the outdoor terrace is the perfect place to rest
  and linger awhile after this delightful walk.

WALK HIGHLIGHTS

Chew Lake and Blagdon Lake are the best known reservoirs south of Bristol.
Much more secretive are the Litton Lakes, two reservoirs built in 1850 by
the Bristol Waterworks Company as a line of works to bring water from
the Mendip Hills to the city. Naturalists will love this walk with the banks
of these reservoirs being home to all manner of flora and fauna ranging

Short Walks near Bristol & Bath

from bluebells, knapweed and primroses to heron, kingfisher and tufted duck. The Lower Reservoir is a shallow, tree-lined 8 acre lake, whilst the 11 acres of the Upper Reservoir are very different in character, being long and narrow with steep sides and fed at the far end by the River Chew.

THE WALK

1 From the Litton car park, drop down some steps by the chestnut tree to a road. To the right are two lanes; follow the left-hand lane for 70m to a gate on the left at the entrance to St Mary's Church and churchyard. Walk through the churchyard to a gate in its far left corner, drop down some steps and join Back Lane. Turn right and, at a T-junction in 200m, turn left along a road shown as Whitehouse Lane on the OS map.

2 In 650m, at a junction by the entrance to Sherborne Farm, turn right into a cul de sac lane. Beyond a cottage, continue along a footpath for 40m before turning left off the main path to cross a stream and reach a gate and stile. Cross the stile and follow the right edge of the field ahead to a gate in its right corner. Follow the right edge of the following field to the next gate, pass through a gate on the right and walk ahead across the Lower Dam below the Lower Reservoir. Turn right and follow a path along the Lower Reservoir that climbs uphill in 350m to reach the Upper Dam and Reservoir.

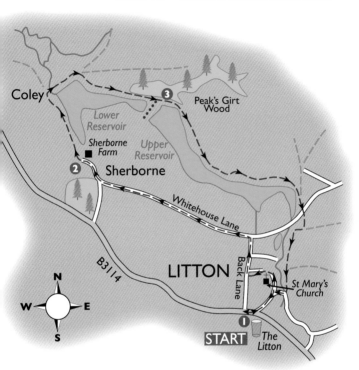

3 Detour to the right across the dam to get an excellent view of both reservoirs; for the main walk, follow the path alongside the Upper Reservoir for 0.5km to a gate and the road by a Wessex Water complex. Turn left and, in 15m, follow a footpath on the right up to a stile. Enter a field, turn right and walk along to a gate in its far right corner. Follow the right edge of a second field to the next gate, before crossing one final field to a gate and stile leading into the village of Litton. Follow the road to the right and, at an early junction, keep left. In 20m, climb some steps on the left back into the car park.

16 Chew Valley Lake & Nature Trails

2½ miles (4 km)

Start: Chew Valley Lake North Car Park, Walley Lane, Chew Magna.
  Postcode: BS40 8SZ.
Parking: Chew Valley Lake North Car Park.
OS Map: Explorer 155 Bath & Bristol. **Grid Ref:** ST574614.
Terrain: Flat and easy walking. Dogs are not allowed on the Bittern Trail on account of its more sensitive habitats.
Refreshments: Salt & Malt, an award-winning fish and chips restaurant and takeaway, is located in Chew Valley Lake North Car Park.

WALK HIGHLIGHTS

Chew Valley Lake, a vast man-made reservoir, supplies much of Bristol with its water supply. It is a haven for anglers and sailors, birdwatchers and walkers. The walk follows the edge of the lake along to a pair of adjoining nature trails known respectively as the 'Grebe Trail' and the 'Bittern Trail'. The names say it all – so don't forget to bring a pair of binoculars.

THE WALK

1 From the car park, turn left (with the lake on your right) along a gravelled path that borders Chew Valley Lake. Follow this path for 600m through to the next picnic area and car park. At the far side of this car park is the start of the Grebe Trail. At an initial fork, follow the gravelled path to the left across grassland. Continue through some woodland and on across open ground, keep on the path as it bears right and walk as far as a junction by some small ponds. Turn left, cross a bridge over Hollow Brook and follow a path to the right down past wooden fencing to an old streambed. Cross this streambed and follow the Bittern Trail to the right.

2 Follow this path, it soon bears left and almost immediately right, along to a footbridge and raised causeway. A detour to the right just before the bridge will bring you to a hide. For the main walk, follow the raised causeway until it ends at a junction. Turn left, and follow a path along the rear of some woodland, open fields to the right, to the junction passed earlier. Turn right, cross the streambed and turn right up to the wooden fencing. Follow the path back up to the bridge over Hollow Brook to reach a junction with the Grebe Trail. Take the left-hand fork, and follow the gravelled path back along to the car park and picnic area. Walk through the car park and retrace your steps along the gravelled path alongside Chew Valley Lake back to Chew Valley Lake North Car Park.

Short Walks near Bristol & Bath

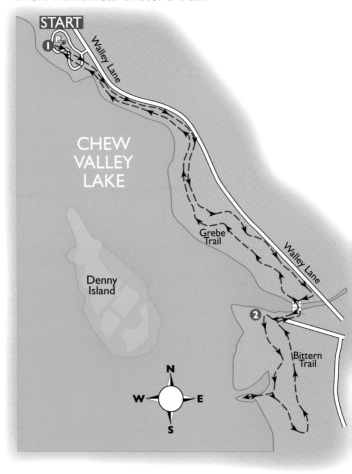

START

Walley Lane

CHEW VALLEY LAKE

Denny Island

Grebe Trail

Walley Lane

Bittern Trail

N
W   E
S

17 Wookey Hole & Ebbor Gorge

3 miles (4.8 km)

Start: St Mary's Church, High Street, Wookey Hole, Wells.
   Postcode: BA5 1BS.
Parking: There is roadside parking alongside the church. Do not park in the show caves car park opposite which is strictly for visitors to the complex.
OS Map: Explorer 141 Cheddar Gorge & Mendip Hills West.
   Grid Ref: ST533476.
Terrain: One steep ascent up through Ebbor Gorge, some 150m of climbing. Three stiles, accessible for all except large, less mobile dogs. Keep dogs on leads on the viewpoint above Ebbor Gorge.
Refreshments: The Wookey Hole Inn is a laid back gastro pub, that draws on influences from the local caves as well as the old-world, new-age Glastonbury.

Short Walks near Bristol & Bath

WALK HIGHLIGHTS

A relatively strenuous walk from Wookey Hole, with its show caves, that includes Ebbor Gorge, a fine example of a Mendip Valley. There is an exhilarating scramble up through the gorge itself, which youngsters will thoroughly enjoy. High above the gorge is a fine viewpoint that overlooks huge swathes of the Somerset Levels as well as bringing a glimpse of Glastonbury Tor. This National Nature Reserve is typical of limestone country; the gorge was carved out by an ancient river that has long since disappeared beneath the permeable limestone. There are small caves along the way where the remains of reindeer and bears, wolves and lemmings have been found by archaeologists.

THE WALK

❶ With your back to the church, follow the road to the right towards the Wookey Hole Paper Mill. Keep on the road as it bears left and, in 275m, immediately past a bungalow on the right called Elm Batch, turn right through a handgate and walk up past this property into the corner of a field. Turn left and walk along the bottom left edge of this field for 275m to a gate and stile at the entrance to the Ebbor Gorge National Nature Reserve. In 275m, ignore the stepped path on the right signposted to Priddy, keeping ahead for another 20m to a right turn signposted to 'The Gorge'.

❷ Follow this path for 275m before scrambling up through the gorge to reach a T-junction by some tree trunks. Turn right and walk uphill for 100m to a junction. The walk now turns left but initially detour to the right for 200m to reach a clifftop viewpoint with a fine view over Ebbor Gorge. Retrace your steps back to that junction and continue ahead for 300m to a gate. Continue on uphill through bramble and gorse to open grassland and the next gate by an Ebbor Gorge Information Board. Continue ahead around the left edge of a hilltop field to a pair of gates and a water trough in the first corner of the field. Do not pass through either gate – instead bear right and follow the line of the hedgerow (on the left) across the hilltop to a stile.

❸ Continue across the next field to a gap in the field boundary and enter the next field, a stile on the left bearing the legend 'Smile on you Crazy Diamond'. At this point, turn right and drop downhill to a stile to the left of a gate. Continue downhill in a second field to a stile before dropping

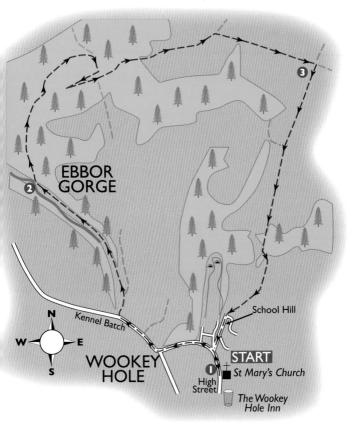

downhill to a gap in the trees at the bottom of a third field. Veer left through these trees to another stile before dropping downhill to the far right corner of one final field to a pair of gates by some trees and the top end of a cul de sac lane (School Hill). Follow this lane downhill to a junction before turning left back to the church and the Wookey Hole Inn.

18 Crook Peak

2½ miles (4 km)

Start: Webbington Road viewpoint & car Park, Webbington Road, Compton Bishop. **Postcode:** BS26 2HB.

Parking: Having passed the New Inn at Cross, continue for another 1¾ miles until, just past Compton Bishop, the Crook Peak parking area on Webbington Road is on the left-hand side.

OS Map: Explorer 141 Cheddar Gorge & Mendip Hills West. **Grid Ref:** ST393551.

Terrain: One gradual ascent onto Crook Peak, with a gentle rocky scramble to secure the summit. No stiles or roads, which means a perfect walk for dogs, but have a lead to hand in case of sheep on the hilltops.

Refreshments: With no pubs or cafés on the walk, take a picnic to enjoy on Crook Peak. The nearest pub is the New Inn at nearby Cross, a dog-friendly pub with a decent beer garden.

WALK HIGHLIGHTS

There is just the one 'peak' marked on the OS maps that cover the Bath and Bristol region and that is Crook Peak. Its height of just 628 feet above sea-level belies its prominence, due to the landscape all around being virtually at sea-level. Indeed, the Bristol Channel is just 6 miles to the west. The summit is marked by magnificent limestone outcrops, giving a genuine mountain feel to this lofty hilltop perch. The views are as you might expect, extending from the Bristol Channel and the Welsh Hills beyond to the Quantock Hills, the Somerset Levels and Glastonbury Tor.

THE WALK

❶ Cross the road to an information board and, ignoring the gate and path beyond this board, turn right to another gate before joining an enclosed track. Follow this track for 400m to a point where it climbs uphill to join an open grassy path coming down from Crook Peak. Avoiding the temptation to turn left and climb the ridge, cross over and follow a track opposite, before bearing left into some woodland and dropping downhill to a junction. Keeping to the lower right-hand path signposted to Compton Bishop, continue for 40m to a gate.

❷ Immediately before this gate, bear left up to a barrier before continuing along a footpath that runs along the bottom edge of the National Trust's

Short Walks near Bristol & Bath

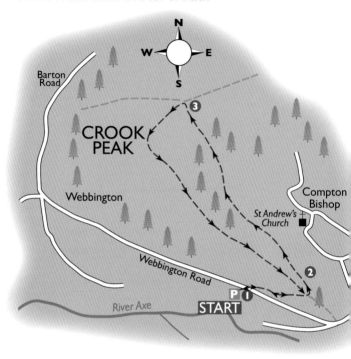

Crook Peak property, with views across the village of Compton Bishop and towards Wavering Down to the right. Follow this footpath as it climbs uphill to reach a dip in the hilltop in 800m. Ahead is a hilltop wall.

3 Turn left and follow a wide grassy track for 250m to reach Crook Peak with its rocky outcrops, an easy rocky scramble just before the final ascent. Follow the grassy ridge that runs south-east from the summit, once again passing above Compton Bishop, to reach a barrier in 1.2km. Beyond this barrier, turn right along a track for 400m back to a handgate, information board and the parking area.

19 Goblin Combe

2½ miles (4 km)

Start: Goblin Combe Car Park, Cleeve Hill Road, Cleeve.
   Postcode: BS49 4PQ.
Parking: The car park is on Cleeve Hill Road just past a left turn called Plunder Street.
OS Map: Explorer 154 Bristol West & Portishead. **Grid Ref:** ST459653.
Terrain: Flat easy walking through Goblin Combe itself, before a climb onto the clifftops where dogs and any youngsters should be kept firmly under control.
Refreshments: The Maple on the A370 in Cleeve, has an excellent menu that uses locally sourced ingredients wherever possible. Dogs are welcome outside in the patio garden.

Short Walks near Bristol & Bath

WALK HIGHLIGHTS

From the village of Cleeve in North Somerset, the early part of the walk follows a path through dark woodland that lies beneath cliffs and scree slopes; it has quite an eerie feel. Soon, however, the path climbs out of the gloom onto the clifftops high above the valley. The views are far-reaching and the feeling of openness contrasts with the shady woodland down below. This is in fact a gorge, cut into the limestone by melting snow and ice during the last Ice Age. The site is now a nature reserve owned and managed by the Avon Wildlife Trust. The clifftops are just west of Bristol Airport and its flightpath, and the planes pass so low in the sky that it is possible to literally see the pilots onboard!

THE WALK

1 Walk back towards the A370 and, in 25m, turn right into Plunder Street, initially passing the Goblin Combe Centre. In a few paces, keep left at a fork and follow the driveway ahead along to the entrance to Walnut

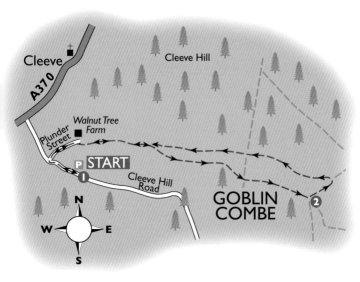

Tree Farm before passing through a gateway into the Goblin Combe Estate. Follow the main path ahead for 1.2km, pass a wall, steps and information board on the left and continue ahead through Goblin Combe. In 400m, ignore a path on the right and keep ahead for another 300m to a junction of paths in a woodland clearing.

② Turn left and, in 150m, follow a faint path on the left that climbs uphill into the woodland. In 150m, continue on this path as it bears right, running parallel to a boundary wall. Continue uphill to a clearing and some farm buildings. Immediately before these buildings, turn left onto a path that passes an information board. Continue for 100m to a stile and open hilltop high above Goblin Combe. Follow the uneven clifftop path ahead and, in 400m, continue on the path as it drops downhill to join a stepped path. Turn left and follow this path downhill back into Goblin Combe, the last part of the path being a steep series of steps. Join the main track that runs through Goblin Combe, turn right and retrace your steps back to the parking area.

20 **Clevedon & Poets' Walk**

2½ miles (4 km)

Start: Clevedon Pier, The Beach, Clevedon. **Postcode:** BS21 7QU.
Parking: There is free parking on the seafront alongside Clevedon Pier.
OS Map: Explorer 153 Weston-super-Mare. **Grid Ref:** ST402718.
Terrain: A generally flat walk that follows tarmac paths, with one
  or two short ascents on the Poets' Walk. A popular walk with dog
  owners, but local bylaws dictate that dogs should be on leads on the
  Promenade.
Refreshments: Clevedon can boast all manner of pubs, cafés and
  restaurants. One of the best is Tiffin at the Beach, located close to
  the pier, with its uninterrupted views of the Bristol Channel.

WALK HIGHLIGHTS
A gentle stroll along Clevedon's seafront from the iconic Victorian pier.
Beyond lies Wain's Hill, now known as Poets' Walk on account of its
association with Coleridge and Tennyson who often walked this way. The

hilltop brings expansive views down the Bristol Channel as well as across to South Wales. And no visit to Clevedon would be complete without a stroll along the pier, described by John Betjeman as being 'the most beautiful pier in England'.

THE WALK

❶ From Clevedon Pier, follow the seafront promenade for 1.2 km along to Marine Lake. Having passed Marine Lake, a popular spot for open water swimming, climb some steps through the woodland at the approach to Church Hill. In 50m, at a junction, turn right to follow a section of the Poets' Walk. In 200m, at a junction by the local churchyard, turn left and walk down to the main entrance to St Andrew's Church. Follow the road opposite down to Old Church Road.

Short Walks near Bristol & Bath

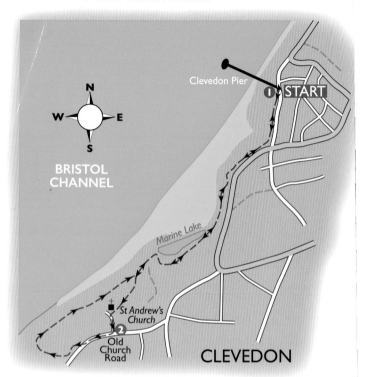

② Turn right and, in 200m, beyond a barrier with a small boatyard ahead, turn right onto a path that climbs up onto Wain's Hill. Follow this path to the south-western tip of the headland, where a seat commands fine views across the Bristol Channel. Continue following Poets' Walk for 1km until it drops back down to the Marine Lake. Retrace your steps along Clevedon's promenade, the reverse walk bringing views to the north towards the Severn Estuary.